Contents

Introduction

The legends about King Arthur are very old. We think they started as stories about a real Celtic war leader who fought against the Anglo-Saxons landing in Britain between the years 400 and 600. A historian, Nennius, wrote about him three hundred years later, when the story-tellers had already had time to add to the truth.

It was perhaps from Nennius that Geoffrey of Monmouth got any facts that there may be in his "history" of Britain (about 1100). But we think the legends were already mixed with the romantic dreams of the story-tellers. Geoffrey of Monmouth added some of his own dreams, we believe.

The stories about King Arthur were told in the west of England, in Wales, and in Brittany. Those are the parts of Europe that the Celts were driven to by people from the north and east.

In the Middle Ages, about 1000 to 1500, there was great interest in romantic stories of the kind the Arthurian legends had become. Writers and story-tellers in several European countries added their own colour. They described the knights and ladies of their own time. Even the castles, armour, lances and shields they described were

King Arthur

and the Knights of the Round Table

Simplified by D K Swan
and Michael West

Illustrated by John James

Addison Wesley Longman Limited,
Edinburgh Gate, Harlow,
Essex CM20 2JE, England
and Associated Companies throughout the world.

This simplified edition © Longman Group UK Limited 1987

First published 1987
Fourteenth impression 1997

ISBN 0-582-54144-1

Set in 12/14 point Linotron 202 Versailles
Printed in China
GCC/14

Acknowledgements

The cover background is a wallpaper design called NUAGE,
courtesy of Osborne and Little plc.

Stage 1: 500 word vocabulary

Please look under *New words* at the back of this book for
explanations of words outside this stage.

those of the Middle Ages, not those of a war leader of a thousand years before their time.

Wace of Jersey, a French writer, added the "Round Table". And legends about other men and women, gods and goddesses, magicians and fairies got changed to make them fit into the King Arthur "cycle" of romances.

People in France and Britain, and in other parts of Europe, began to think up and write their own stories about the knights and ladies of King Arthur's court, One of the best-known British stories of this kind is *Sir Gawain and the Green Knight*. We don't know who wrote it. It was written before 1400 in very fine poetry.

The first book of stories of King Arthur and the knights of his Round Table to be printed was the *Morte d'Arthur* of Sir Thomas Malory. Caxton printed it in 1484 (he had set up the first printing house in England in 1476). It is not in poetry but in very good clear English of the time. It is a putting together of the best-known Arthurian stories of Malory's time. Most of them were translated by him from the French.

The stories in this book are taken from Malory's book. We have made some changes for readers of modern English, and you may be interested to see (with only the spelling modernised) a sentence from page 2:

Whoso pulleth out this sword of this stone . . . is rightwise King born of all England.

Arthur takes the sword out of the stone

Chapter 1
Arthur and Merlin

Once there was a king in Britain called King Uther. He was a great and good king. He loved the beautiful Princess Igraine, and he wanted to marry her, but she did not love him. He was very sad, and everyone thought that he would die.

There was a magician named Merlin. He could change himself into any animal or bird; he could change so that no one could see him. He could go from place to place by magic. One day Merlin came to King Uther. He said, "King Uther, I will help you. You shall marry Princess Igraine, and she will have a son. I will help you if you will give that son to me."

"I will give him to you," said the king.

So King Uther married Igraine, and they had a son. They named the son, Arthur. When Arthur was three days old, a very old man was seen at the door of the king's house. It was Merlin. Then King Uther took the child in his arms and went out and gave him to Merlin.

Soon after that, King Uther became very ill. He knew that he was going to die. Then Merlin said, "Call all your knights and great men and tell them, 'My son, Arthur, will be king after me!' "

King Uther did that before he died. But all the knights and great men began to fight: each wanted to make himself king. Merlin took Arthur

1

away. He gave the child to a good knight named Sir Ector. Arthur grew up with Sir Ector's son, Kay, and became a man.

When Arthur was a man, Merlin went to the archbishop (the head of the Church) and said, "Call all the great men of Britain to London. Then they shall see the man who will be their king."

All the great men came to London. They went into the church, and the archbishop spoke to them. When they came out of the church they saw in front of the church door a great stone. There was a sword in the stone, and there was writing on the stone:

THE MAN WHO CAN TAKE THIS SWORD OUT OF
THE STONE IS THE KING OF BRITAIN

All the knights tried, one after another, to take the sword out of the stone, but none of them could do it. The sword would not come out.

At the same time there was a great joust in London. All the great knights jousted in it. They began on their horses with spears. They rode quickly, and met – CRASH! Some knights fell off their horses, and then they fought on foot with swords.

Sir Ector went to the joust with Sir Kay and Arthur. The two young men wanted to joust, but Sir Kay had no sword. Arthur said, "There is a sword in a stone outside a church. I saw it on the way here. I'll get it and fight with it, and you can have my sword, Sir Kay."

They rode to the church. Arthur got off his horse; he took the sword in his hand – and it came out of the stone.

They went back to the field. When Sir Ector saw the sword, he kissed Arthur's hand and said, "You are my king."

They went to the archbishop. Then the archbishop called all the knights.

The archbishop said, "Put the sword back into the stone." Arthur put the sword back into the stone. All the knights tried again to take it out, but it did not move.

Arthur took it out again. So they cried out, "Arthur is king! Arthur is king!"

They all went into the church, and the archbishop made Arthur King of Britain.

So Arthur became king. He married the most beautiful lady in England, Princess Guinevere, and she became his queen.

Then Merlin made the Round Table.

There were one hundred and fifty places at the table. Each knight had his name written in his place. There were one hundred and twenty-eight knights at the table. As time went on other brave and good knights came, and King Arthur gave them places. One place was not filled for a long time. That place was for a knight who had never done any bad thing to anyone. It was called the "Seat Perilous": if a bad man sat in it, he would die. After many years Sir Galahad came and was given that place.

Chapter 2
The sword, Excalibur

King Arthur went all over the country, getting to know his people and helping them. After many days he came to a great forest. He was still in the forest when evening came. Then he saw in front of him a castle. It was the biggest and most beautiful castle he had ever seen.

As he came nearer, the great door of the castle opened and a lady came out.

She said, "King Arthur, I ask you to stay in my castle. Night is near, and you must have food and a bed."

"I thank you," said King Arthur, and he went in.

After they had eaten, Queen Annoure told one of her men to lead the king to his bedroom.

Next morning Queen Annoure said, "I'll show you my castle and all the beautiful things that I have in it. I have more jewels and gold and riches than any living person."

They went from room to room, and each room was richer and more beautiful than the last: Queen Annoure was a magician. Then they came out on to the top of the castle. The queen said, "See those beautiful gardens and all those green fields. They are all mine. And see that great wall on all sides. Stay here with me and be king of all this. You can't get away: the door of the castle is shut, and that great wall is on all sides. And my men stand ready to make you stay or to kill you if I tell them to do so."

King Arthur said, "I think nothing of your magic. Your servants can't kill me and they can't make me stay."

Then, with his sword in his hand, Arthur went out of the castle, and out through the door in the great wall. Nobody could stop him.

The house of Sir Pellinore was not far from the castle of Queen Annoure. Queen Annoure sent a man to him, saying, "A very bad knight is coming to my castle. He wants to kill me and take my jewels and my gold. He is on his way near your house. Go out and fight him, and save me."

So Sir Pellinore came out against King Arthur. He rode against the king with his spear, and Arthur was thrown from his horse. Then they fought with swords. They fought on – and on. Then the king's sword broke.

"Ha!" cried Sir Pellinore, "you have lost the fight."

Arthur threw down his broken sword; then he ran at Sir Pellinore, and took him in his arms; he threw him down on the grass and set his foot on his head.

Arthur took off his helmet. Sir Pellinore looked up and saw his face. "It's the king!" he cried. "I didn't know." He told Arthur what

Queen Annoure shows King Arthur her castle and gardens

Annoure had said, and they were friends.

King Arthur had broken his sword in the fight against Sir Pellinore. Merlin came to him and said, "Come with me, and you shall get the best sword that was ever made. It's a magic sword."

The king went with Merlin through the forest. The trees shut out the daylight, and Arthur could not see the sky. After a long time they came to an open place where there were no trees, but a lake of water. As Arthur stood by the lake he saw an arm with a sword in its hand come up out of the water.

"Go and take it," said Merlin. "It is the sword Excalibur. It was made for you by the Lady of the Lake, who lives in her home in the water of the lake."

There was a boat at the side of the lake. King Arthur got into the boat and went and took the sword. The scabbard of the sword was covered with jewels.

"That is a magic scabbard," said Merlin. "No man can kill the man who has it."

There was a queen named Morgan le Fay. King Arthur did not know that she was a magician and an evil woman. He thought that she was good, not evil, and that she was his friend.

One day he went out riding in the forest. He took his spear, but he did not want to take his sword. He gave Excalibur to Queen Morgan le

Fay, saying, "I will come and get it on my way back."

Arthur rode on in front of the men who were with him. He lost his way in the forest. When night came, he was alone. He saw a little light and rode to it. Then he saw that the light was in a beautiful ship on a lake. The ship was near the side of the lake, so he went on to the ship, and he saw food and drink on the table and a bed, all ready.

"I'll stay here tonight," he said. "In the morning I'll find my way back, and get Excalibur, and go home."

So King Arthur ate, and slept. But, when he woke, he saw that he was not in the ship. He was in a little room with a very small window. The door was shut: he could not get out. There were three other men in the room. They were knights.

They said, "This is the castle of Sir Damas. He is a very evil knight. He caught us and put us here, saying, 'You may go out if you will fight for me. If you will not fight for me, you will stay and die here.' "

Men came and led Arthur into a great hall in which Sir Damas was sitting.

"Will you fight for me?" Sir Damas asked.

King Arthur said, "I'll joust for you if you will give me those three knights. Give me those three knights, and, after I have fought for you, we shall all go back to our homes."

"Yes," answered Sir Damas. "You can have the three knights if you will fight for me."

Then a man came into the hall and said, "Queen Morgan le Fay sends King Arthur his sword, Excalibur."

King Arthur was very glad to have his sword. He made ready to joust.

When Arthur came out to the jousting field he saw another knight waiting there. There was no mark on his shield showing who he was, and his face was hidden so that Arthur could not see it.

The fight began. King Arthur was unhappy: his sword Excalibur did not bite on the other knight's shield. Then he knew that this sword was not Excalibur; it was some other sword made to look like Excalibur.

He fought on. Then Arthur's sword broke.

The other knight said, "Say that you have lost the fight, and I will not kill you."

"No!" cried Arthur. "I will fight on – and on."

Then Arthur hit the knight on the head with his broken sword – so hard that he fell down and his sword fell from his hand. Arthur quickly took the other knight's sword. It was Excalibur!

The knight had at his side the scabbard.

Arthur took the scabbard; then he said, "Tell me who you are. What is your name?"

The knight answered, "I am Sir Accolon, Knight of the Round Table."

"Why have you fought against me, your king?"

He answered, "I didn't know that you were King Arthur. I thought that you were Sir Damas. Queen Morgan le Fay said to me, 'King Arthur is in the castle of Sir Damas. You must go and fight Sir Damas and save your king.' And she said, 'Here is King Arthur's sword, Excalibur, and its scabbard. Take them for the fight so that you may save your king.' "

King Arthur rode with Sir Accolon and the three knights against Sir Damas. There was a great fight, which King Arthur won.

Sir Damas was brought before the king.

"Why did you do this thing?" said King Arthur.

"Queen Morgan le Fay told me to do it," answered Sir Damas.

Then the king said, "You are no knight. You shall not have a sword or shield. I take from you your castle and all that you have and give them to your younger brother."

Morgan le Fay was at Camelot while Arthur was away. She heard that King Arthur was alive. She went to Queen Guinevere and said, "I must go back to my own country. My people want me to go back to them."

Queen Guinevere answered, "Don't go. The king will soon be here. He will be glad to see you." (Queen Guinevere did not know what Morgan le Fay had done!)

"No! No!" said Morgan le Fay. "I must go. I must go now." And she rode away alone on her black horse.

Morgan le Fay rode her black horse all that day, and all the night. She asked all the people she saw, "Where is King Arthur? Tell me, where is the king?"

At last she saw a man who said, "The king is ill. He had a hard fight at the castle of Sir Damas, and he is now in the House of the Good Women."

The Good Women worked for God and gave help to people who were ill or poor.

Morgan le Fay rode on and came to the House of the Good Women. She said, "I have come from far away. I have been riding day and night. Please give me food."

They brought food to her.

"Is there any other person here, in this house?" she asked.

They said, "Yes. King Arthur is here. He is sleeping."

"Oh! The king!" she cried. "I cannot stay to speak with him: I must go on. But may I look at him? May I see his face? I love him so much! I will not wake him."

The Good Women said, "Yes, you may go and look at him, but don't make a noise. Don't wake him."

Morgan le Fay went into the king's room. She stood at his side as he slept. She saw that the king had his hand on the sword, Excalibur: she could not take it away without waking him. Then she saw the scabbard at the foot of the bed. She took it and hid it in her clothes and went out of the room, and got on her black horse and rode quickly away.

The king opened his eyes; he saw that the scabbard had gone. He called the Good Women and said, "Did anyone come into this room when I was sleeping?"

They said, "Queen Morgan le Fay came – but no other person. She could not stay to speak with you, but she wanted to look at your face because she loves you so much."

"I thank you," said the king. "Thank you for having me here in your house. You have been very good to me. I must go now. I must go after Queen Morgan le Fay. She has taken the scabbard of Excalibur."

He was still not well, but they could not make him stay. So the Good Women helped him to get on his horse, and he rode away.

He rode on, and on. At last he came to a river. There was a man there with his cows in a field. The king asked, "Has anyone come this way?"

"Yes," answered the man. "A beautiful lady came on a black horse. She went across the river here, and she rode on, very quickly."

King Arthur went over the river and through a forest, and up a hill. Then he looked down, and he saw Morgan le Fay far away.

Morgan le Fay looked back and she saw the king. She rode on, over a place covered with stones, then down a hill to a lake. The water in the lake was black. No animal drank it. No birds sang in the trees.

She got off her black horse and took the scabbard and threw it far away into the water.

"King Arthur shall never have it!" she cried. "That scabbard shall not save him from all who fight against him. No one will ever find it there!"

Then she rode away.

King Arthur came to the place. He could not see Morgan le Fay or know which way she had gone. He could not see the marks of her horse's feet because of the stones.

So Morgan le Fay went back to her own country and stayed there.

King Arthur had the sword Excalibur, but the scabbard was never found.

Chapter 3
Vivien and Merlin

When King Arthur was young, Merlin the magician helped him in every way. He showed him how to be a good king and a brave knight. He helped him to rule well, so that all the people loved him. He helped him to build the beautiful city, Camelot. But Merlin became old, and he knew that Arthur must help himself and do without the help of magic. He said to Arthur, "I shall not be with you much longer. I shall go down alive into a cave, and I shall not be able to come up out of it to help you."

Arthur said, "Can't you save yourself by your magic?"

"No," answered Merlin. "I can't. What must be, will be."

The Lady Vivien came to Camelot. She had lived with the Lady of the Lake (who made Excalibur). The Lady of the Lake was a great magician, and Vivien knew all her magic. When Vivien knew all the Lady of the Lake's magic, she went to Camelot and worked with Merlin. When she knew all Merlin's magic she thought, "Now I know more magic than Merlin. He is an old man; I can't kill him, but I can shut him up somewhere. Then I shall be the greatest of all magicians."

Vivien went with Merlin to a far country

Merlin goes into the cave with Vivien

where there was a great hill of stone. In it there was a magic cave.

Merlin told Vivien, "The mouth of the cave is open now, but if you speak magic words they can make it shut."

"What are the words that will make it open again?" asked Vivien.

"I don't know," said Merlin. "I know how to make the door of the cave shut, but I don't know how to open it again."

"I want to go into the cave," she said. "Come in with me."

So Merlin went into the cave, but Vivien ran quickly out, and said the magic words. The mouth of the cave shut, and Merlin could not get out.

Some men say that he is still there. One day, they say, somebody will break open the cave and he will come out and help us all with his magic to be good and happy.

So Arthur had no more help from Merlin.

Chapter 4
Sir Meligrance

It was the month of May, and the fields were full of flowers. The queen called her ten knights and said, "We will go into the fields and get flowers, and my ladies shall come with me."

So they all rode out into the fields. When evening came, the queen said, "Now we'll go back to Camelot, to King Arthur."

As they all made ready to go, twenty men in armour came out from the forest. Then their leader cried out, "Stand where you are – or you will be killed."

It was Sir Meligrance. He loved Queen Guinevere and wanted to take her away to his castle.

The queen said, "King Arthur made you a knight: how can you do this thing to his queen?"

The ten knights said, "We have no armour, but we'll fight against your men who have armour. We will not see our queen taken away without a fight."

The ten knights could not stand against men in armour. They were all wounded, and they would have been killed, but the queen cried out, "I can't see my knights killed before my eyes. Don't fight any more, but come with me to Sir Meligrance's castle."

So they all rode to the castle, but, as they went, the queen called to her side a boy who had a very good horse. She said, "Take this ring. Ride and take this ring to Sir Lancelot and tell him to come and save me."

Sir Meligrance saw the boy ride away. He told his men to catch him, but they could not.

Sir Lancelot got on his horse and rode to the castle of Sir Meligrance. When he came near the castle he thought, "Sir Meligrance will hide his men near the road, and they will come out at me as I ride by. So I will not go along the road, but will ride through the forest."

It was as Lancelot had thought. Sir Meligrance hid men by the road, but Sir Lancelot did not come that way.

Sir Meligrance saw Lancelot coming to the castle. All his own men were far away, waiting by the road. Then he was afraid. He went to Queen Guinevere and said, "Oh, queen, forgive me for what I did. Forgive me this time. I will bring you back to Camelot and I will fight for King Arthur as a good knight."

The queen did not know that he had seen Lancelot and that he said this because he was afraid. So she answered, "I forgive you."

When Lancelot came into the castle the queen said, "I have forgiven Sir Meligrance. Stay here tonight. We'll go back to Camelot in the morning."

Sir Meligrance knew that Lancelot was still

angry. He knew that Sir Lancelot would fight him and kill him as soon as the queen had gone.

They sat down to eat in the great hall of the castle. When they had eaten, Sir Meligrance said to Lancelot, "I'll lead you to your room."

Then he led Lancelot into a room where there was a door in the floor. Sir Lancelot put his foot on the door, and it opened and he fell into a little room far down, from which he could not get out. Then Sir Meligrance went and said to the queen, "Sir Lancelot did not want to stay here. He has gone back to Camelot."

The queen went back to Camelot, and King Arthur said, "What is this thing that your knights tell me? They say that Sir Meligrance took you away to his castle?" And he said to Sir Meligrance, "What is this thing that the queen's knights are saying?"

Sir Meligrance answered, "I didn't take the queen away. She came with me because she loved me."

Then the king was very angry.

There was a girl in Sir Meligrance's castle. She carried food to Sir Lancelot every day. She saw how strong and brave he was. When Sir Meligrance had gone to Camelot she opened the door and Sir Lancelot went out and rode back to Camelot.

The king was sitting with the queen and his

knights in the hall when Sir Lancelot came in. He went up to Sir Meligrance and said, "You took away Queen Guinevere to your castle. For that she forgave you, so I shan't kill you for that. Then you said that she came with you because she loved you. For saying that I shall kill you. I am the strongest of all King Arthur's knights, so I'll fight without armour against you in your armour. Even so, I shall kill you."

So it was. Sir Meligrance came at Sir Lancelot with his sword and struck down at his head because he had no helmet. But Lancelot jumped to one side, and with his sword cut Sir Meligrance's helmet in two. And Sir Meligrance fell dead.

Chapter 5
Sir Tristram

One day the King of Lyonesse was lost in the forest. The queen was soon going to have a child. When the king did not come back from his riding, she ran out into the forest to find him. She went a long way, and at last she fell at the foot of a tree. There she had her little son. She knew that she was going to die, so she kissed the child and said, "Ah, little son, your coming has been sad, so your name shall be Tristram, but you will grow up to be a brave and good knight." ("Tristram" means "sad one".)

The king's men found the queen and the child in the forest and took them back to the castle.

For many days the king did not speak or eat, and men said, "He will die too, and the little child will be our king." But at last the king began to live again.

After seven years the king married another queen. The new queen had a son. She loved her own son very much, but she did not want Tristram. She wanted to kill him.

The queen got some poison and put it ready for Tristram to drink when he came back from riding.

"He'll die when he drinks it," she thought.

But the queen's son came in before Tristram

and drank the poison, and died.

Again she got poison and set it ready for Tristram, but the king came into the room. He put his hand out to take the poison, but she cried out, "Don't drink it!"

Then the king remembered how her son had died, and he knew what she wanted to do. He said, "You wanted to poison Tristram, but your son drank the poison. So again you set poison for Tristram, but I was going to drink it."

Then he told his servants to take the queen and make a great fire and burn her.

The fire was made ready. Then Tristram threw himself down at his father's feet and said, "Father, do not do this thing! Take her back, and love her, and she will love you and be a good queen; but send me away."

Then Tristram went and lived with his father's brother, Mark. Mark was King of Cornwall. Tristram grew up and became a very brave and strong man.

Sir Marhaus was the son of the King of Ireland, he was very brave and strong. He was the strongest of all knights. No one could stand against him in a fight. He came in his ship to the castle of King Mark and he said, "Say that you will be my man and do all that I tell you to do, or send one of your knights to fight me."

Not one of King Mark's knights would go to fight Sir Marhaus. They knew that he was too strong. Then Tristram said, "I am not a boy now: I am a man. Make me a knight and send me."

At last King Mark said, "I do not want to send you, but I have no other man to send."

So Sir Tristram and Sir Marhaus fought. They fought all day. Sir Marhaus was strong, but he was older than Sir Tristram, and he was not so quick on his feet. Tristram was younger and very quick, Sir Marhaus could not hit him. The sun was hot, and, as the day went on, Sir Marhaus did not fight so strongly. Then at last Tristram's sword cut through Sir Marhaus's helmet and wounded him in his head so that he died, and his men took him away to his ship.

Sir Tristram was wounded too. It was a very bad wound. There was poison in it and it stayed open and did not heal.

No one could make Sir Tristram's wound begin to heal. At last an old woman came and said, "The poison in the wound came from Ireland. You must send Sir Tristram to Ireland. There someone will make it heal."

So King Mark sent Sir Tristram in a ship to Ireland, but Sir Tristram called himself by another name, because he had killed Sir Marhaus, son of the King of Ireland.

Tristram played the harp very beautifully. The King of Ireland heard him playing as his ship came near, and he brought him to his castle. He told the Princess Isolt to heal Tristram's wound.

So Isolt made Tristram's wound heal, and Tristram showed her how to play the harp. They were very happy, like brother and sister.

There was a knight named Sir Palamides. He loved Isolt and asked her again and again to marry him. She did not like him, and she told him to go away, but he would not go. He made her very unhappy. There was a joust and Sir Palamides came to it. He had black armour and a black shield, and he rode a black horse. Tristram got white armour and a white shield, and he rode a white horse. He rode at Sir Palamides with his spear, so that the black knight fell over the back of his horse. Then Tristram stood over him with his sword and said, "Go away from here and don't speak to Isolt again – or I will kill you!"

Sir Tristram went back to Cornwall. He told King Mark about Isolt and how good she was. Then King Mark said, "I have no wife. If I marry Isolt, the King of Ireland and I will be friends, and there will be no more fighting. It will be good for my people if I marry Isolt. Go and ask the King of Ireland to give me Isolt to be my queen."

So Tristram went to Ireland. The King of Ireland said, "Yes, it will be a good thing for this country and for Cornwall." And he sent Isolt to King Mark.

Tristram took Isolt on his ship to go to Cornwall. The ship came to Cornwall and he said sadly, "I am going away to Camelot to become a Knight of the Round Table and fight for King Arthur, but if ever you want my help, I will come."

One day when Isolt was walking in the forest, Sir Palamides came and took her up and put her on his horse and rode away. Another knight rode after him. Sir Palamides heard the knight coming, and he got off his horse to fight. Then Isolt ran away. She went on and on through the forest. Night was coming on, and there was no help. Then she saw a lake, and she said, "I'll throw myself into the water and die, then I shall be saved from Sir Palamides."

Just as Isolt was going to throw herself into the lake she heard someone coming. It was a knight named Sir Atherp. Sir Atherp saw Isolt standing there, and he said, "Can I help you? Why are you alone in the forest, with night coming on?"

She answered, "I ran away from Sir Palamides. He'll come through the forest and catch me and take me away. Oh, save me from him!"

Sir Atherp said, "Come with me into my castle. I'll save you from Sir Palamides."

So Sir Atherp led Isolt to his castle.

Soon Sir Palamides came riding through the forest and came to the door of the castle. The

Tristram shows Isolt how to play the harp

door was shut. He cried, "Open the door!" but no one answered.

Sir Tristram was riding on his way to Camelot. A man ran and told him, "Sir Palamides has taken Isolt away on his horse." Then Tristram came quickly back. He found a knight wounded in the forest and took him to a hut. It was the knight who had fought Sir Palamides.

"Where did Isolt go?" Sir Tristram asked the wounded man.

"I don't know where she went," answered the knight. "She ran away when she saw us fighting."

Sir Tristram went on and saw a lake. He saw the marks of feet near the water, and the marks of a horse. He went on and came to a castle. The door of the castle was shut, and outside the door of the castle he saw Sir Palamides.

Sir Palamides saw Tristram and rode at him. But Sir Tristram's spear sent Palamides back over his horse on to the grass. Sir Palamides stood up and took his sword. Then Tristram got off his horse and took his sword, and they fought with swords there in front of the castle. Isolt looked down from a window and saw that Tristram had come to save her. She saw Palamides fall and she saw Tristram stand over him, and she cried out, "Don't kill him!"

Sir Atherp's men opened the door of the castle and she ran out. She said, "Don't kill him,

Sir Tristram. He fights bravely. Send him to King Arthur and he will become a good knight and fight for others, not for himself."

So Sir Palamides went to Camelot, to King Arthur, and he became a very good knight, and all men said good things about him.

Sir Tristram brought Isolt back to King Mark, and he stayed in Cornwall for some time.

Now King Mark began to be afraid of Sir Tristram. He thought, "Sir Tristram is young and brave. He fought twice against Sir Palamides and saved my Queen Isolt from him. Now she will love him, and will not love me."

One day Tristram was sitting with Isolt near the sea. He was playing on his harp, and Isolt was happy hearing it. Then King Mark came out at him with a sword and killed him, and he fell dead at the feet of Isolt.

Day after day, Isolt sat looking out over the sea. She would not eat or drink or speak. And so she died too.

King Arthur heard what King Mark had done, and he sent a knight, who came to Cornwall and killed him.

Chapter 6
The Grail

One day an old man dressed all in white with a white beard came to King Arthur and said, "Oh, king, I have brought a young knight to you. He is the son of a great man and he will do great things."

The king looked and saw a young man standing there in red armour; and his face was very beautiful.

You have read about the Seat Perilous: it was a place at the Round Table where no knight could sit if he had ever done any bad thing to anyone. If any bad man sat in that place, he would die. Each knight had his name written on the table in his place, but in the Seat Perilous there was no name.

The old man led the young man to the Round Table, to the Seat Perilous. There was a name there – where there was no name before. It was written in gold: SIR GALAHAD.

"Sit here," said the old man. Then he went out from the hall and was never seen again.

"Who is this young man who has sat down in the Seat Perilous and is not afraid?" the king asked. "Does anyone know him?"

"I know him," said Sir Lancelot. "As I rode towards Camelot I came to a House of Good Women, and the Good Women brought out this young man to me saying, 'His name is Galahad. You must make him a knight.' "

Then many of the other knights looked at Galahad, and they saw that his face was like the face of Sir Lancelot. They remembered that, when Sir Lancelot was very young, he was married. They thought, "That's Sir Lancelot's son." But Sir Lancelot did not speak to the young man as a son.

As the knights sat there at the Round Table they heard a great noise. Then there was a great white light. They looked up and saw the Grail covered with a red cloth... And then it had gone!

For a time no one spoke. Then Sir Galahad said, "That is the Grail. Jesus drank from it on the night before He died. Now I know that the Grail is in this country, and I will go out and look for it. I will not come back without finding it."

Three other knights said this same thing: they were Sir Lancelot, Sir Bors and Sir Percivale.

King Arthur was very sad. He said, "We were all brothers, but now our Round Table is broken. You will go, and I shall not see you again."

So the four knights rode away. For many years they looked for the Grail and did not find it.

Many other knights rode away looking for the Grail, and did not find it, and some never came back. The Round Table was not as it was: in the evening, when the king and queen sat there,

The knights of the Round Table see the Grail

there were many unfilled places. And King Arthur was very sad.

After many years Sir Galahad and Sir Percivale and Sir Bors came to a place near the sea. They looked down from a hill and saw a ship. It was evening, but the ship was full of light – white light, like the light of the sun – and they knew that the finding of the Grail was near.

They went down to the sea, and then they went into the ship. There, on a table, Galahad saw the Grail.

Then a great sleep came on them. The ship went out to sea. When they opened their eyes they saw that they had come to a city.

Sir Galahad said, "We must take the table and the Grail out of the ship."

So they took the table and the Grail into the city.

The king of that country was very ill. He died, and the people did not know whom to have as a king after him. The great men were sitting in the city-hall to find a new king. Then an old man came into the hall – an old man dressed all in white with a white beard. He said, "Take as your king the youngest of these three knights who have come to your city. He shall be your king." Then he went out from the hall, and no one saw him come, or saw him go.

Sir Galahad was made king.

Sir Bors went back to Camelot. Sir Percivale lived alone, giving himself to God.

Sir Galahad did not live long. He said, "I have seen the Grail, and I am happy. I do not want to live long."

He built a beautiful church and put the Grail in it.

Soon after that the same old man came to him and said, "Your work is done. God calls you."

In the morning they found him in front of the Grail, dead. And his face was very happy.

Chapter 7
King Arthur dies

King Arthur was angry with Lancelot. Lancelot went over the sea to France, and King Arthur and Sir Gawain went there to fight him.

While Arthur was out of England, an evil knight named Sir Mordred came to Camelot and said to Queen Guinevere, "King Arthur has gone out of the country and he is dead. I am now king, and you must be my queen."

Then Guinevere ran away to the Tower of London, and all her men went with her. Mordred came, but the walls were very strong, and he could not break in.

Soon Mordred heard that King Arthur was coming back to England with many ships and with all his men. So Mordred went with all his men, and there was a great fight. Sir Mordred's men could not stand against King Arthur: they ran from the field. But Sir Gawain was wounded. He said to King Arthur, "I am dying. Give me a pen and paper so that I may write to Sir Lancelot." He wrote:

To Lancelot, bravest of all knights.

Today I was wounded in the fight, and I know that I am dying. Because of the love that we had for each other, come quickly and help King Arthur.

He asked Arthur to send this quickly to Lancelot,

and then he died.

Sir Mordred got more men and came to a place near the lake where Arthur had gone with Merlin to get Excalibur, and there King Arthur came against him.

On the night before the fight, Arthur saw Gawain in his sleep. Gawain said, "Don't fight Mordred now. After one month Lancelot will come with all his men and help you, and save the queen."

When the king awoke, day had come. He called his knights and said, "There will be no fighting today. I shall go and speak with Mordred. Come with me. Bring your swords, but they must stay in their scabbards. If Mordred or any of his knights puts his hand to his sword, then fight and kill!"

A man came and told Mordred, "King Arthur is coming to speak with you. Tell your knights this, 'Your swords must stay in their scabbards. If any man puts his hand to his sword, then the king and his knights will fight and kill.'"

King Arthur stood speaking with Mordred. All King Arthur's knights stood near him, and Mordred's knights stood near Mordred.

As they stood there, a snake came out of the grass and bit a knight on his foot, and he took his sword to kill it. Then, seeing one knight put his hand to his sword, all the knights began to fight.

They fought all day. When evening came, the king saw that two of his knights, Sir Lucan and

Sir Bedivere, were alive. Sir Lucan was badly wounded. All the others were dead, and Mordred stood with his sword alone: all his men had been killed. Then the king ran at Mordred with a spear, and the spear went through his body, but, as Mordred fell, he wounded King Arthur with his sword.

Sir Lucan and Sir Bedivere took the king to a little church which stood near the field. But, as they came there and set the king down, Sir Lucan fell and died of his wound. And Sir Bedivere was alone.

Then King Arthur said, "I must soon die too. So take my sword Excalibur, and go to the lake and throw it into the water."

Sir Bedivere said, "I will do it." So he took the sword, but, as he walked to the lake he saw the jewels on it, and he thought, "If I throw this beautiful sword into the lake, what good will that do?" So he hid Excalibur by a big stone, and went back to the king, and said, "I have done what you told me to do. I have thrown your sword into the lake."

"What did you see there?" the king asked.

"I saw the water, and the sky, and the stones. That is all."

"You didn't do as I told you," King Arthur said. "Go again, and throw Excalibur into the water, and come back and tell me what you saw."

Sir Bedivere went again to the lake and took the sword from its hiding place. But as he looked at it and saw how beautiful it was, he thought, "I can't throw this sword into the water. It shall be at my side so long as I live, and I shall remember King Arthur." So he hid it again, and went back to King Arthur, and said, "I have thrown Excalibur into the lake. I saw the water, and the stones and the sky, and I saw the sword fall into the lake."

"Go again," the king said very sadly. "If you don't do it this time, I'll kill you with my hands."

So Sir Bedivere went again. He took the sword from its hiding place. Then he threw it far over the water. An arm came up out of the water and caught the sword, then took it down into the lake. Sir Bedivere went back and told the king what he had seen.

"Now," said King Arthur, "take me to the lake."

So Sir Bedivere took the king down to the lake, and, when he came there, he saw a black ship at the side of the water. In it there were many ladies, all dressed in black.

As he looked at their faces, he thought, "These are the faces of many women whom I have known, women who have died but are still remembered."

King Arthur said, "Please put me on the ship." So Sir Bedivere set him down in the ship, and the ladies stood round him.

The ship went out over the water, and Sir Bedivere stood there alone.

Sir Bedivere sees an arm in the water catch the sword

Questions

Questions on each chapter

1 Arthur and Merlin
1 What was Uther?
2 What was Merlin?
3 Who married Igraine?
4 Who gave Arthur to Sir Ector?
5 What was in the stone, and what was on the stone?
6 What could none of the great men do?
7 What did Sir Kay and Arthur want to do?
8 How many times did Arthur take the sword from the stone?
9 Who became King Arthur's wife?
10 What would happen if a bad man sat in the Seat Perilous?

2 The sword, Excalibur
1 Who lived in the castle?
2 What happened to King Arthur's sword in the fight with Sir Pellinore?
3 Where did Arthur first see the sword Excalibur?
4 Who was Morgan le Fay?
5 Where did Arthur go to sleep?
6 And where did he wake up?
7 How did Sir Accolon get Excalibur?
8 Where was Morgan le Fay while Arthur was at the castle of Sir Damas?
9 Where was the king after the fight?
10 What did Morgan le Fay take away?

3 Vivien and Merlin
1 Who helped the young Arthur?
2 Who wanted to be the greatest of all magicians?
3 What did Vivien do when Merlin was in the cave?
4 Why couldn't Merlin get out of the cave?
5 What do some people believe about Merlin?

39

4 *Sir Meligrance*

1 Why did Sir Meligrance want to take Queen Guinevere to his castle?
2 What did the boy carry from the queen to Sir Lancelot?
3 What did the queen not know when she forgave Sir Meligrance?
4 Where did Sir Meligrance go from his castle?
5 How did Sir Lancelot get away from the castle?

5 *Sir Tristram*

1 What did "Tristram" mean?
2 Whose son was Sir Tristram?
3 Who drank the queen's poison?
4 Where did Sir Marhaus come from?
5 What happened to Sir Marhaus?
6 Why didn't Sir Tristram's wound heal?
7 What did Sir Tristram teach Isolt?
8 Who married Isolt?
9 Why didn't Sir Tristram kill Sir Palamides?
10 What happened to Sir Tristram in the end?

6 *The Grail*

1 Who brought Sir Galahad to King Arthur?
2 Who already knew Sir Galahad?
3 What was the Grail?
4 Who were with Sir Galahad when he found the Grail?
5 Which of them went back to Camelot?

7 *King Arthur dies*

1 Why did King Arthur go to France?
2 Why did Queen Guinevere go to the Tower of London?
3 What did Sir Gawain ask Sir Lancelot to do?
4 Why did one of the knights put his hand to his sword?
5 What did all the knights do after that?
6 At the end of the day, who was alive on Mordred's side?
7 When did Sir Lucan die?
8 Where did Sir Bedivere hide Excalibur?
9 What happened when he threw Excalibur into the lake?
10 Where did Sir Bedivere put King Arthur?

Questions on the whole story

These are harder questions. Read the Introduction, and think hard about the questions before you answer them. Some of the questions ask for your opinion, and there is no fixed answer.

1 Story-tellers have added magic to the King Arthur stories. What was the magic part of:
   a the sword in the stone? (page 2)
   b the Seat Perilous? (page 3)
   c Excalibur? (pages 7 and 37)
   d the scabbard of Excalibur? (page 7)
   e the cave in the far country? (page 15)

2 Merlin:
   a What magic things could he do?
   b How did he help Arthur to be a good fighter?
   c How did he help Arthur to be a good king?
   d What, in the end, could he *not* do?

3 The good ones and the bad ones:
   (The page where the name comes *first* is in brackets.)

   King Arthur (1)   Sir Meligrance (17)
   Sir Ector (2)   Sir Lancelot (18)
   Queen Guinevere (3)   Sir Tristram (21)
   Queen Annoure (4)   Isolt (24)
   Sir Pellinore (5)   Sir Palamides (24)
   Morgan le Fay (7)   Sir Galahad (29)
   Sir Damas (8)   Sir Mordred (34)
   Vivien (14)   Sir Bedivere (36)

   a Can you name two men who were wholly good?
   b Can you name one woman who was wholly evil?
   c Can you name one man who was wholly evil?
   d Can you name two women who were wholly good?
   e Can you name one man who was bad but became good?

4 Sir Galahad:
   a What did he look like? (Page 29 may help you to answer.)
   b Why was he not afraid when he sat in the Seat Perilous?
   c Why did he leave Camelot?
   d Where did he find the Grail?
   e Where did he put the Grail?

5 Which of the stories did you like best? Can you say why?

New words

armour
   iron pieces to cover the
   head, body, arms and legs
   of a knight

castle
   a place with strong walls
   that soldiers can hold

evil
   very bad

Grail
   the cup Jesus used at the
   "Last Supper" (see page 30)

harp
   a musical instrument with a
   lot of strings

heal
   make (a wound) better

helmet
   an iron covering for a
   knight's or soldier's head

joust
   fight, knight against knight,
   as a sport; a meeting for
   jousting

knight
   a horse-riding leader of
   soldiers

lake
   a small sea with land all
   round it

legend
   an old story about great
   men, magic, etc, of long
   ago. A legend may perhaps
   have grown around some
   real person or happening.

poison
   something (often a liquid)
   that may kill a person

romance
   love and adventure, often in
   a far-away time or place
   where life seems happier or
   more exciting than it really
   is for most readers. Adj:
   romantic.

scabbard
   the cover for a sword

shield
   an iron-covered frame
   (often with the knight's own
   mark on it). A knight
   carried it on his arm, and
   used it to stop another
   knight's spear or sword.

snake
   a long creature without legs,
   often with poison in its bite

spear
   a long piece of wood with
   an iron point at one end